T0368533

The Cursillo, How's Your 4th Day?

Ryan Lee Nevins

Edited by Dennis Lyons

Copyright © 2022 Ryan Lee Nevins.

All rights reserved. No part of this book may be used or reproduced by any means, graphic, electronic, or mechanical, including photocopying, recording, taping or by any information storage retrieval system without the written permission of the author except in the case of brief quotations embodied in critical articles and reviews.

This book is a work of non-fiction. Unless otherwise noted, the author and the publisher make no explicit guarantees as to the accuracy of the information contained in this book and in some cases, names of people and places have been altered to protect their privacy.

Archway Publishing books may be ordered through booksellers or by contacting:

Archway Publishing
1663 Liberty Drive
Bloomington, IN 47403
www.archwaypublishing.com
844-669-3957

Because of the dynamic nature of the Internet, any web addresses or links contained in this book may have changed since publication and may no longer be valid. The views expressed in this work are solely those of the author and do not necessarily reflect the views of the publisher, and the publisher hereby disclaims any responsibility for them.

Any people depicted in stock imagery provided by Getty Images are models, and such images are being used for illustrative purposes only. Certain stock imagery © Getty Images.

THE GIDEONS INTERNATIONAL:
"Copyright © The Gideons International. All rights reserved."

ISBN: 978-1-6657-1381-8 (sc)
ISBN: 978-1-6657-1382-5 (e)

Library of Congress Control Number: 2021921041

Print information available on the last page.

Archway Publishing rev. date: 1/22/2022

Dedicated to all those that kept and keep this movement moving!

The Cursillo,

The Cursillo is a "Short course in Christianity" that was founded by Roman Catholic laymen

In 1944 in Majorca, Spain while they were trying to improve ways to train pilgrimage Christian leaders.

It is a three day movement that is used to show Christian lay people how to become successful Christian leaders. The primary objective is to ask the Cursillo participants or "cursillistas" to take back into the world and practice what they have learned which is called their "4th Day". It is followed up with "Ultreya's!" which is Spanish for "Onward!" where cursillistas share their practical experience with what they have learned. Since 1944 the Cursillo movement has spread all over the world and is used by many other sects and denominations.

The Cursillo, How's Your 4th Day?

1. Seek God with all your heart

Seek God with all your heart
give Him all you got and you will never be apart
He will stay by you and continue to watch over and lead
all you have to do is be willing grow like a mustard seed

When you put God first and make Him a priority in your life
everything seems to turn out all right
but when you chase all those empty things
misery is created and a sad song you sing
but if you seek first the Kingdom of God
Good fortune will follow and your soul will enlarge
with God's love that will put a smile on your face
when He is your master of your race and not in 2nd place

Refrain

God wants you to love Him so
and when you bless others your relationship will grow
He wants you to love Him first
then to love your brothers and sisters as you love yourself and to not cause hurt
selfishness might seem like it leads to gain
but in the end comes suffering and pain
that is why you must begin to start
trusting Him so you do not feel separate or apart

Refrain

If you seek God with all your heart
His spirit will flow into you right from the start
all you have to do is ask and you shall receive
and remember faith without works is dead so do good deeds
and the seeds you plant will blossom and grow
and in time peace, love and happiness you will know
so trust Him that lives in your heart
and let Him guide you and a new day will start

2. Masks (Know yourself)

We all have masks that we choose to display
but underneath it all is a child that has something to say
and wants to talk about the hurts inside
so He can emerge from underneath all the false pride

God made all of us unique human beings
with work to complete before it's time for leaving
and to accomplish this we must be ourselves
and not compare and contrast to anyone else
Since before the beginning of time God has had a plan
that all may be one and that we may be instruments of peace on his land
and our job is to play our part
and be true to ourselves and come from the heart

Refrain

It is hard to be vulnerable when we have experienced much pain
and it is hard to trust when our faith in people have been drained
after years of getting hurt we can build a wall that stands tall
to protect ourselves from having any falls
but the more bricks that we lay the more we experience delay
and feelings aren't processed and we don't mature the right way
but with the help of God and our brothers and sisters
in time we can take each one down if we aren't resistant

Refrain

It takes courage to let down your guard and risk it all
but living in fear is not living at all
hardships and pain are a part of life
but together we can get through the darkest of nights
God will shed the light and always lead the way
so we can experience a brighter day
and if we take of the masks that we wear and get to know ourselves
we will find underneath our true selves

3. Who is God for me today?

Who is God for me today?
definitely not the God of yesterday
He is the one who loves me unconditionally and fulfills me
He is the one full of grace the puts a smile on my face
when along trudging along this journey and trying to finish the race

When I was young God was someone that I had
on my team who made me feel joyous and glad
I had a purpose and a reason to live
a calling to answer and something to give
but along the way choices that I made led me astray
and from Him I felt very far away
the distance was long even though He dwelled inside
and when He would talk to me but I would not reply

Refrain

My life became dark and so did my conception of Him
I was angry and I lived a life full of sin
my actions were not in line with His will
I was empty inside and that void I tried to fill
but only with things that were not good for me
and I lost myself and the truth was hard to see
but then God would appear in my life
and I would realize He was always there especially in the darkest of nights

Refrain

God carried me when I thought I was alone
He was always there helping this sheep find his way home
so I could be together and part of the flock
and never did He give up and never did He stop
He gave me chance after chance
so I could regain my footing and maintain my stance
and because of all my experiences Who is God for me today?
God is love who is always directing me the right way

4. Need to love need to be love

We need to love and we need to be loved
and if we want to be connected to God above
we have to develop and nurture a relationship with Him
by reaching out our hand so the friendship can begin

We all have needs and they need to be met
for if we aren't given the proper love problems we start to get
we go outside ourselves to get our emotional needs filled
and in the end it leads to pain and a life unfilled
nobody can fill that need more than God
and if we love Him first by accepting His invitation we will never starve
we will get the love that we need if we trust and believe
and seeds of happiness will grow into trees

Refrain

Loneliness is the absence of love
and no matter what you have nothing can be in replace of
you can have all the wealth and material gain
but with out love life is empty and full of pain
but with God in your life you are filled with joy
happiness you will experience when His ways are employed
and if you keep on loving Him and continue to do the right thing
God will bless you and a new song you will sing

Refrain

When there is intimacy and you reveal who you are
God will accept and love you unconditional with all bruises and scars
His love for us is limitless and we are never out of reach
and the Shepard will go to any length to retrieve a sheep that weeps
He loves us so much and He wants us to know
that He is their for us wherever we go
He wants to lead us to the promised land
and as friends do walking hand in hand

4

5. Don't be too hard on yourself

Don't be too hard on yourself be gentle and kind
Because we all make mistakes from time to time
Just learn from them and give yourself a break
So you can grow as a person and progress you can make

None of us are perfect and we all make mistakes
No one of us are walking on water so we let self-forgiveness take
Because that is the only way to get better
And when we are understanding it will be the ladder
That allows us to climb to new heights
And reach right where we should set our sights
And to be like Jesus and which is how He would have us be
But to get their we will surely make mistakes but we must learn from them then let them be

Refrain

God is gentle, loving caring and kind
And He wants us to treat ourselves the same way so we can find
Peace, joy and happiness in our lives
Because when we beat ourselves up we are guaranteed to lose the fight
There is no gain in this kind of pain
It only leads us to misery and depression when in this mind frame
So relax and take it easy on yourself
And let the self-love be felt

Refrain

Those who practice self-compassion make more progress
They do better than those that are hard on themselves when problems need to be addressed
So the best way to go is to let the love flow
Be good to yourself so peace you know
And above all your worth it and God doesn't make junk
So put down the bat and use the feather and heal those lumps
And in the end more progress you will see
When you are not being too hard on yourself and you let our friend be

6. Persevere is to love

Persevere is to love
It is to rise above
Any situation, conflict or upsetting grudge
And to choose to abide to God's will
And continue to keep moving forward until the struggle is nil

We must do our best to do God's will
We are called to love no matter what our enemies deal
We must take the high road and carry our load
No matter how devastating the episode
How we react and stay intact
Is more important than any pay back
So to stay on track we must cut some slack
And turn the other cheek and take the impact

Refrain

It is hard to practice our faith
And keep God first and let all sin be erased
There is much temptation and it is easy to fall
That is why we must stick together so we remain to stand tall
Because without God and each other we are destined to fail
But when two or more gather in His name all will prevail
God's love is the glue that will hold us together
That's why we must put Him first so we can persevere through the stormy weather

Refrain

To succeed we must walk in love indeed
It is not an easy path and it takes courage to lead
And Along the road less traveled you might feel alone
But God is always with you and He will let it be known
So while you're trudging on your way back home
Keep your eye on the prize and remember you reap what you sow
And most importantly persevere is to love so be an instrument and keep on the go

7. Impact on others

You may have on impact on others and not even know it
That's why you must continue to practice your faith and grow in it
So when people look at you they see the spirit of Christ in your eyes
And the existence of God cannot be denied

Whether we know it or not we have an effect
What we say and do causes others to reflect
And think about the messenger and their message
That is why we must do our best to go in the right direction
And practice our faith and live and love
And let God work through us and let His light shine us as He guides us from above
So we can be instruments of His peace
And be an example of power to all those who seek

Refrain

How we carry ourselves is evident to others
How we walk and talk can lead others to discover
The reality of God that is deep inside
That is why we must do our best to be true and abide
Because we may be the one God uses to get inside
The soul of one that is hurt and vehemently denies
That is why we must do our best
To give hope too all that are in distress

Refrain

God is love and we must love too
And show everybody what He can do
And the way we live our lives
May be the difference to those lost in the night
So be the light and shine bright in this dark world
And you might help someone even though the impact on another may not be known to you

7

8. God doesn't ask us to be successful just faithful

God doesn't ask us to be successful just faithful
And we can do that by being obedient and grateful
And doing the best with our God given abilities
But most important serving Him with humility

We are called and we all have a purpose
And if we ask God for direction you can count on that He heard us
But the answers will come in His time
That is why we must relax until them we find
And when we do it is our job to
Give our best effort and let God's plan ensue
And leave all the results up to Him
So no matter what happens we all will win

Refrain

God calls us all to serve
He gives us our talents so He can be seen and heard
It is up to us to make the most of them
And if we have lived up to our potential there is peace within
That is why we must do our best
So we can lay our head on the pillow at night and quietly rest
Knowing the truth inside
That we did our best and in that we should take pride

Refrain

It is in the effort not the outcome and knowing we have done our best
Because if we have done our best a healthy sense of pride will reside in our chest
Knowing that we gave God our all
even though short we may have fall
But the victory is in the attempt
Though disappointment we may have to accept
We can still look in the mirror and stand tall
Knowing that we have succeeded in being faithful and giving our call our all

9. God loves us even when it doesn't seem so obvious

God loves us even when it doesn't seem so obvious
When trouble is around and we are surrounded by darkness
But never despair because God is always there
To shine His light letting you know for you He loves and cares

God knows the amount of number of hairs on your head
He knows everything from when you wake up until you go to bed
He has a unique plan for your life
So remember everything happens for a reason when the night darkens your sight
Keep the faith and know He is always around
To protect you when you don't feel safe and sound
He also has Guardian Angels to protect and care
So remember you are never alone when never despair

Refrain

God is with us every step of the way
He walks with us and if we are in dismay
He will carry us until we are safely home
In Heaven where all the Angels and Saints serve and roam
And though life can be bleak and we may experience defeat
God will help us get back onto our feet
So we can continue trudging along to our final destination
Where only love is experiences plus joy and elation

Refrain

God is Our Father and He loves and cares
No matter what He will always be there
He is loving and caring and gentle and kind
Even when we have our trials that test our heart and our mind
But we find in the end when we look back
That God is our friend even when faith we lacked
And though at times it might have been so obvious
God loves us that is why we must continue to trust

9

10. People are instruments of God's Grace

People are instruments of God's Grace
He uses us to put a smile on a sorrowful face
He sets us up and puts us in the right place with another
So we can look at each other and with affection and call ourselves sisters and brothers

People are the tools God will use
To get His work done and spread the Good News
He takes people that are down on the ground
Totally defeated and lifts their spirits until their feet are on the ground
And they are able to walk and talk about their life
To give hope to another who has fell behind

Refrain

God works in mysterious ways
And there are so many ways that He displays
His love for us when we are depressed and down
When we feel discouraged and our heads are pointed towards the ground
But the people He puts in to our life
Are no coincidences they were planned with foresight
By a God who cares for us so much
And wants us to be at peace before we return to ashes and dust

Refrain

God is the conductor and we are His instruments
And when listen to His commands harmonious music we are gifted with
And when we abandon ourselves totally to Him
We are sure to succeed and destined to win
So when we are called to be an instrument of God's Grace
We must answer the call because people cannot be replaced

11. God is with us all the time

God is with us all the time
Even in the darkest of places His light continues to shine
For sinners like you and me
That need to overcome pain and misery

God is always there with love to spare
He cares for us especially when we start to despair
Whether we are having good or bad times we are never alone
He is there to help us on our journey Home
All we have to do is speak
Call out His name and His love will reach
To any place in this universe
So keep the faith when life starts to hurt

Refrain

This too shall pass nothing does last
Especially life which goes by real fast
But as we continue to walk in faith
God is with us setting the pace
He guides us as we travel this foreign land
And if we ask Him He will hold our hand
And when we look back sometimes we will only see
One set of footprints and that is when we were carried by Thee

Refrain

God is love and no matter what we are loved by Him
No one is forsaken no matter how grievous their sins
God is compassionate, understanding and kind
And if we look deep within we will find
The truth that God is always there
He dwells inside the temple of every child He bears
So if we start to feel that we are all alone
We must remember God is there all the time wherever we rome

12. Words hurt but they can heal

Words hurt but they can heal
So choose them wisely and consider how someone feels
Because they can do damage in assortment of ways
But most of all they can heal so we must think and be positive in what we say

Words are powerful they can change a life
They can bring about a metamorphosis as radical as dark turning to light
They can bring sight to the blind and direction to those who are lost
But if we use them improperly we will pay the cost
Words can cause pain and emotionally drain
When people are callous and spiritually inane
That's why we should think before we speak
Because harsh words can emotionally cripple and cause another to weep

Refrain

When words are properly used
And not to scorn, belittle or abuse
They can turn a life from one that is full of dismay
To one that is happy, joyous and gay
But if we stray from there proper use
And don't use them with love everyone is destined to lose
But if we let God work through us and have His say
We all win in the end because we did it His way

Refrain

God gave us a brain and a heart to use
And when we collaborate and combine the two
Nothing is impossible when we let God work through
And show what he can do
And when we don't neglect love and respect
Peace and harmony is what we get
So even though words can hurt we must remember they can heal
And if we get the opportunity like Jesus we should be gentle when it comes to how others feel

13. Palanca

Here is your Palanca to show support and care
Letting you know you are not alone and that God is there
Also people that are there for you
To guide you on your journey and pray for you

Congratulations on your reintroduction with Christ
And stepping out of the darkness and into the light
Know that only God wants the best for you
And He loves you and has a wonderful plan for your life so always be true
He has brought you this far so keep the faith
Continue on your journey no matter how high the hills that you face
And even though life is not always easy and at times is hard
Remember you're never alone and He is never too far
He is with you every step of the way
until you are safely Home forever with you He will stay

Refrain

God is merciful and God is fair
He is understanding to the crosses that you bare
He wants you to depend on Him to carry your load
So offer them up to Him as you journey on the less traveled road
And you will realize that your cross is your gift
As your experiences can give others spirits a lift
And the hope they need to overcome and succeed
Which makes you so grateful you say thank you Jesus on a bended knee

So go ahead and enjoy the ride
Abide in God and you will feel His peace and joy inside
Let it reside in you and put a smile on your face
And let the perpetual light shine down upon you and experience His Grace
So you can have part of Heaven on earth
And on your 4th day be an example of God's handiwork
And say God don't make junk and you are worth it to those who are hurt
But above DeColores! so the joy of Jesus you exert!

DeColores!.

Ryan Lee Nevins+

14. You got a friend in Christ

You got a friend in Christ
He's always nice and you don't have to ask Him twice
He hears every word you say
And will respond to you in His own special way

Christ is your best friend
He suffered and died for you and He will come again
But until then He is there to help
So get on your knees and ask and His love will be felt
He cares so much for you
and there is nothing that He wouldn't do
so put your trust in Him
and watch a true friendship begin

Refrain

Christ has risen from the dead
And He can resurrect your spirit with the blood He shed
He gave all so you could stand tall
Have the shame and guilt wiped away that came from your falls
He's full of love, compassion and forgiveness
And there are plenty of people that stand as a witness
To the greatest story ever told
Of a man who laid down His life for His friends who didn't fold

Refrain

Christ is love and Christ is caring
He came for the sinners who were despairing
He forgave all and said go and sin no more
And never turned away a person who knocked on His door
So remember when your full of doubt
All that Christ did and that He is there to help you out
So you can experience freedom and release
From your cares and worries but most importantly peace

15. Piety

Piety is aiming one's whole life towards God
so we must stay focused and aim for the stars
and make are goal to make it back to Heaven
where everything is perfect like the number seven

Being pious means that we do the best that we can
To better man or woman
It is to live up to our potential and use the gifts that we have
To glorify the one that gave us life and made us human
God only as progress from us not perfection
Everyone falls short of the glory of God except the one who experienced the ascension
So if we sin we must be forgive ourselves
And be gentle so God's love is felt

Refrain

When on the road less traveled we will make mistakes
We will do things that make ours and others hearts to ache
But if we repent for our sins and mend our ways
The Lord will forgive us and mercy will be displayed
But if we continue to be neglectful and cause harm
Then we shall reap what we sow and the pain lingers on
But God loves a tryer so no matter how many times we fall
He will help pick us up so we can again walk tall

Refrain

Prayer, meditation and service to others
And being part of the Church which is our sisters and brothers
It Is fundamental in growing in our faith
But most importantly is loving God and our neighbor as ourselves which sums up our faith
And if we practice that we can live in harmony with each other
And if Thy will is done happiness we will discover

16. Actively seek God out

Actively seek God out by doing His will
Do unto others as you would have them do unto you
And you will see in the end you will find
The happiness you have been looking for all of the time

When we put the word of God into action
It fills our souls and brings us satisfaction
Nothing can compare to the rewards we receive
When we trust and believe and then sow some seeds
The key is to be diligent in our work
And to remain humble with our outlook
Then we will feel God's presence in our lives
Which will wake up our spirits and make us feel alive

Refrain

God wants us to do good things with our lives
He wants us to use our talents so we can enjoy them, help others and He can be Glorified
Never does He want us to waste
What He has given us that could put a smile on someone's face
He wants us to be the best we can be
And to contribute to the world abundantly
Whether it is a kind word or saying hello
There are no small contributions so let your love show

Refrain

If we are trying there is no denying
God is happy with our efforts that we are applying
The most important thing is that our heart is in the right place
And that we think of others and applaud we don't chase
We must do our good deeds for the right reason
Which is love and compassion which never goes out of season
So if we want happiness we must actively seek God out
And then we will know what life is all about

16

17. A time for everything

There is a time for everything in God's universe
A time for joy and a time to hurt
A time to laugh and a time to cry
And we will experience it all before we die

There is a time and a place for everything under sun
And in life as we are on our journey and have work to get done
We all will have our ups and downs
Times we lost and then again found
So we must not dwell on all the defeats
But use them as stepping stones to reach new feats
And continue to compete and rise above
And carry our cross and depend on God's love
To get us to the end where we want to be
Which is Heaven where love and peace flow freely

Refrain

Timing is always key
And when it is God's time nothing can be done more perfectly
Because God always knows best
At first it might make sense but hind sight will show His finesse
God is in control even when it seems not so
And if we learn to let go and Go with His flow
Good things will eventually come to pass
Above all His love that will always last

Refrain

So we must keep the faith in Our Fathers time
And be patient as we continue to grind
And as we experience our hardships and successes
We will be better if we let God impress us
By letting Him show what He can do
When we choose to surrender and follow through
And if we answer His call the sun is sure to shine
We just need to be patient and follow the signs
Because there is a time for everything in this life
And if we keep God first no matter what we will be alright

18. Daring of the soul to go where it does not see

Daring the soul to go where it does not see
Takes courage and trust in Thee
No one knows where the road will lead
But if we take a leap of faith in good hands we will be
But most importantly we will fulfill our destiny

If we are to succeed we must have faith in God
We must trust Him even though it might be hard
There will be definitely critics along the way
That will think we are crazy but God works in mysterious ways
And makes heroes out of the least expected people
because they had the courage to follow Him even though their sight was feeble

Refrain

God believes in us so we must believe in Him
We must do our best to pick up our cross and follow Him
What He asks might not be easy and we shall have our falls
But He is always there to pick us up so we can stand tall
Because He loves us so much it is beyond comprehension
And if we decide to open up and let Him in
He will show us the way and lead us down the right path
Where happiness is found all we have to do is ask

Refrain

Doubt and fear might crowd our soul
But if we keep the faith God's plan will unfold
Our responsibility is to keep moving forward
In the direction that God has ordered
And humbly serve and abide
And do our best to walk the straight line
And if we do God will have a surprise
Which is everlasting love, joy, peace and happiness on the other side

19. Head or heart full of faith

Do you have a head or a heart full of faith?
Is it your head or your heart that you depend on to set the pace
Because when you let your heart direct you to finish the race
Success will be yours if your heart takes first place

Knowledge is power but where does it come from
Is it something you thought of or does it come from the Holy One
Because when you acknowledge Him He shall direct your paths
So trust in Him at all times and good things will come to pass
And when you trust your heart over your head you will find
You can have confidence that you are in line with the Divine
And though you may make some mistakes
It will lead to progress if chances you take

Refrain

The head can be tricky and it is easy to get confused
But if you listen to your heart you will hear the Good News
And God will lead you to the promised land
Where peace of mind is never in demand
That is why you must be still and listen to His voice
And though those around you disagree with your choice
You must stand firm and keep the faith
Knowing that in God's time everything will fall in place

Refrain

True knowledge comes from the source
And when you depend on just your head you become divorced
From God's wisdom that wants to show you the way
With His everlasting light to a brighter day
and though it may be scary and it takes courage to trust in the Divine
and moments of doubt you will experience and bouts surrendering to His plans and designs
everything will be fine if you have a heart of faith
because it will always lead you past the finish line straight to Heaven's gates

20. Choosing good or evil

Choosing good or evil may seem like an easy choice
But when sin calls it can make you ignore the voice
That is deep inside which is God talking to you
Saying to stay on the road less traveled even though it is the harder thing to do

When we are at the crossroads and we have to make a choice
To listen to our conscience which is God's voice
Or fall into the enemy's trap of temptation
Where sin is appealing not showing the path to degradation
But if we choose to take the higher road
It might be harder but we will reap good if that is what we sow
And peace and happiness is what we will come to know
If we pray for the strength and choose to follow

Refrain

It is easy to give into temptation
And ignore the consequence we will be facing
But if we continue down the wrong path
The day becomes night real fast
And darkness clouds our souls and our minds
And we lose ourselves and become hard to find
And time goes by not knowing where it went
And we wake up one morning with remorse and regret

Refrain

But if we choose to do the right thing
And trust God a joyous song we will sing
Our view of life and of ourselves
Will be positive so we must aim where the Angels and the Saints dwell
And do the best that we can
To follow Christ but always remember that we are human
And that we are going to make mistakes
But God will always love us no matter how many wrong turns we make
And help us get back on the right road
So we can get safely home

21. Dynamic encounters with Jesus

While on this journey we will have dynamic encounters with Jesus
Joyous moments that never fail to please us
He will surprise us in so many mysterious ways
That will lead to progress and constantly amaze

Jesus always has a trick up His sleeve
That deepens our faith and helps us believe
He works His miracles in many ways
Showing His love for us as we go through our days
And as time goes on our relationship blossoms and grows
And we come to know a love that we never have known
And inside we will feel complete
Because He has enabled us to rise from the ashes up unto our feet

Refrain

Jesus will do whatever it takes to get our attention
He works through numerous ways to show His affection
He will teach us lessons to get on the right road
And He will send help so we can carry our load
Letting us know that He is there for us
And that we are never alone and in Him we can trust
Because He will never bail or fail
But be the wind in our sails to help us prevail

Refrain

Jesus wants to put a smile on our face
He wants us to succeed in the trials that we face
He is always there to lend a helping hand
And hold ours when life seems too hard to withstand
He wants us to grow more in the image of Him
Which is to be loving and caring and have peace within
So He deliver us from sin to a better life
by using dynamic encounters to bring us from the dark to the light

22. The Sacraments

The sacraments are our way of life
They have been given to us as a gift by Jesus Christ
they are a visible symbol of the reality of God
and when we practice them we experience the Grace of God

There are 7 sacraments that are necessary for our salvation
Though not every sacrament is meant for every individual or for every vocation
It starts with Baptism which is the gateway into the church
And frees us from the original sin that was present at birth
Next is Holy Communion also known as the Blessed Sacrament happens at the age of reason
And we celebrate the body and blood of Christ in remembrance to please Him
Third is Confirmation and when the Holy spirit comes down
and we are strengthened as we renew our vows
These are the sacraments of initiation
Where we begin our journey and follow Him to our final destination

Refrain

The Sacraments of service are how we glorify God
The first being marriage when a man and a woman are joined by God
and support each other in sickness or health
and are loyal no matter what life has dealt
second is Holy orders where one is called to preach the word
and give up their life to love and serve

Refrain

Lastly are the sacraments of healing
Which are to help us when we are sick and spiritual, emotional or physical pain we are feeling
when we are guilty of sin we practice penance or reconciliation
Where we confess them and are absolved when we face them
Anointing of the sick is when a priest or a bishop blesses those who are in need
And ask for God's guidance to intercede on behalf of those who plead
These are the ceremonies that we Catholics claim
Will lead us **safely** home to where in which from where we came

23. Love in action

Love in action is practicing what Jesus taught
it is being of service to our brother or sister who is struggling to carry their cross
It is reaching out and lending a hand
like Simon did when Jesus was fulfilling Our Fathers plan

Faith without works is dead
We must take action on what has been said
We must love God and our neighbor like we love ourselves
And to do that we must try to help
All of those that are in pain
That are struggling and suffer the same
And be instruments of His peace
To give release to all those who seek

Refrain

We must imitate Jesus each and every day
And let Him work through us to help those in dismay
We can help people even if we aren't physically there
By using the most powerful weapon against the enemy which is prayer
We can minister to those by talking and more importantly lending an ear
And console those who are living in fear
And remind them that they are never alone
And God will surely be with them until they are safely home

Refrain

There are many ways we can express our love
And be witnesses of the Lord up above
But no matter what challenges we face
The most important thing is to have our hearts in the right place
Because that is what matters to God
How we treat each other when times are hard
And when we put love in action
It will bring the most joy and satisfaction
Plus Jesus said what you do to the least of my brethren you do to me
so we should be quick to help those in need

24. Obstacles

What are the obstacles standing in my way
Preventing me to be the best person I can display
Who and what are bringing me down
Making it hard for me to be mentally, physically and spiritually sound

What are the obstacles in my life?
What is making life a harder fight?
What is clouding my vision making it harder for me to see?
What is making me tired and weary?
We have to find out and address
All of the things that cause our worry and stress
So we can find a solution to them all
by offering them all up to God after we have hit a wall

Refrain

There are so many things that can cause setbacks
But setbacks can lead to comebacks if we change how we act
If something isn't working for us we need to make a rearrange
Because if we don't our lives will stay the same
So we must take an honest look at ourselves
And remove all the dust from the shelves
So our house can be clean and neat
And make all of the clutter obsolete

Refrain

Life is a struggle and it's hard enough
Without making the battle more rough and tough
The best thing we can do is trust in the Divine
And be still and know everything will be just fine
Because it is when we are impatient that we trip over our feet
Stumble to the ground and experience defeat
So in order to not repeat we must be victorious
By overcoming all of our obstacle so our lives can be more peaceful and harmonious

25. Believe in yourself

Believe in yourself and say I can
Do anything that God has planned
For me to achieve in this life
And He will give me the courage and the strength to win the fight

God gives us all talents and gifts
To share with the world and He does insist
That we develop them to the best of our ability
And shine like stars and do it with humility
Taking credit for only the effort we put in
And giving the rest of it to Him
And being grateful for what we have
And the joy we experience because of what we add

Refrain

No talent is greater or less than
They are all needed and when we embrace them
Joy comes into are lives
Plus a heightened self-esteem that beings our spirit to life
Confidence then comes our way
When we get approval for what we display
And at the end of the day if we have done our best
We can walk away peaceful with pride in our chest

Refrain

When we believe in ourselves and we say I know I can
We can build our dreams if we trust ourselves and that we are in Good hands
And though we may have set backs we will be able to complete
Any task that we need to finish if we don't have an attitude of defeat
But the most important quality of them all
Is confidence in ourselves that we can answer any call
That God has for us
So we can win in the end and be victorious

26. Can't please everyone

You can't please everyone and it's ok to say no
And do what is best for you and not go with the flow
Even though your heart is in the right place
It is not healthy to neglect yourself because imbalance you will face

You might feel guilty if you say no
Or bitterness if you say yes but really don't want to do so
You suppress a lot of emotions like rage, annoyance, stress and grief
And it is hard to get any peace or relief
You can't give entirely of yourself and expect to feel good in the long run
So you must do what is healthy and take care of number 1
And in the end happier you will be
If you put yourself first and think I have to do what is best for me

Refrain

It might seem selfish at first
But self-care is the only way to stop the hurt
There might be pressure to keep up appearance
But only stress is gained by trying to maintain a perfect self-image
Plus you leave yourself open to abusers of all kinds
Narcissists, energy vampires, bullies and other types that are wounded inside
And it is ok to have compassion
But at the expense of yourself is too much to be asking
So you must be true and love yourself
And let go of toxic people until health is felt

Refrain

In the end people pleasing is a selfish act
It is more about controlling how someone reacts
Plus nobody really knows the true you
Because you keep so much locked inside because you fear of being disapproved
The only thing they know is the mask
Not the authentic person that God asks you to broadcast
Plus the desire to be loved and approved
Only backfires making you feeling lonely and unviewed
So be true to yourself and take responsibility for your happiness
Learn to be assertive and it will wipe away the sadness
Feel your feelings and find your self-worth
And always remember you are a child of God who doesn't want you to hurt
But feel His unconditional love inside of you
So no more people pleasing you will do

27. Be liked for who you are

Be liked for who you are and who God made you to be
No need to live a lie or be phony
God made you special and unique and one of a kind
You're a diamond in the rough and the only one of you you'll ever find

God wants you to be true
You have your own song to sing and work to do
It is your job to shine and learn how to refine
And hone your skills in God's time
And be the person you were born to be
So you can enjoy life and be happy
And radiate that energy to others
So they can in turn learn how to discover

Refrain

Everyone is blessed though we are not the same
We all play a different position in the ball game
But that doesn't mean we are better or less
We are all important and need to finesse
Our individuality and be ourselves
And shine like the sun and overcome any darkness that dwells
And do the best that we can
So we can attract serious fans

Refrain

God doesn't make mistakes and He loves you so much
He wants you to take time to get in touch
And be you and not follow what others do
But tread your own path and trust Him as you walk on through
So always remember to be your true self
and that you don't have to be anyone else
and if you do you will be liked for who you are
by the people who accept and love you no matter how imperfect you are

28. God don't make junk (I am Loveable)

God don't make junk you are worth it all
And no matter how many times you fall
God will love you until the last day
So say I am loveable when you look in the mirror everyday

To say there is no good in someone is an insult on God
Everyone has good in them even though it might be hard
To see through years of suffering and pain
That causes one to look at another with disdain
But Jesus came for the sinners and never turned His back
He loved them with all His heart and got them back on track
And treated them with love and compassion
And forgave them for their sins and promised life everlasting

Refrain

Nobody is perfect only the son of God
We are all equal and we all have it hard
Are trials and tribulations might come in different ways
But a cross is a cross and they are all heavy
That is why we must not look down
At any one that is on the ground
Unless we are going to help pick them up
Like Simon did for Jesus when the going got tough

Refrain

God gave you a soul and He wants to restore it to health
He wants to take away your sins so peace is felt
He wants you to live happily
And develop a relationship with Him so it can come to be
Because God doesn't want you hurting inside
And if you surrender with humility and learn to abide
You will receive plenty of gifts
But most importantly the truth that God don't make junk so say to yourself I am loveable and I am worth it

29. Mistake making machine

We are mistake making machines but it's all right
God loves us anyway whether we are in the dark or in the light
The point is to learn from our past
And ask for forgiveness so away our sins are cast

Life is hard and being a Christian is tough
There is a reason that it is called the road less travelled because on it there are not enough
But if we have self-compassion and accept God's grace
Despite our mistakes we can live a life that is Holy and look ourselves in the face
that is why we have reconciliation
to get back on the road that leads to our final destination
and if we are gentle on ourselves
we will make progress from the times we fell

Refrain

God is love and He loves us no matter what
When we fall He is there to help pick us back up
He knows it is hard and doesn't expect perfection
Only progress and that we learn from our lessons
Because God is merciful and forgiving
He is slow to anger and Grace He is always giving
He is not hard on us so neither should we be
Because berating ourselves only causes pain and misery

Refrain

Jesus came for the sinners and He loved them so
He changed their life by showing them which way to go
And was a power of example of how to live life
He forgave His worst enemies and had compassion at the hardest time of His fight
He died for our sins so we can win
Our constant battle of between the good and evil within
And if we humbly admit we are mistake making machines
God will forgive us and render our souls new and clean

30. Look forward not back

Look forward not back so you don't get stuck in a rut
Because if you live in the past you miss out on what is in front
So learn from the past grow and let it go
And look forward to a better tomorrow

It is easy to get caught up in the past
And relive memories wishing those time could of last
Or maybe it's the reverse where times where worse
And you wish you could change the memories that cause pain and hurt
But either way there is nothing you can do
But be grateful for the good times and learn to let go of the ones that disturb you
And focus on what God has next for you in your journey
Which is exciting because we are always still learning

Refrain

The goal is to be present and enjoy the moment
And be grateful for the gifts God has given to us open
Because God never fails to surprise
You never know what is going to happen that can open up your eyes
That is why it's wise to realize
That we need to be here now before time goes by
And we miss out on our lives and experience regret
Which is a hard lesson to forget

Refrain

Life is an adventure and exciting when lived
But if we only live in our minds we miss out on what it has to give
That is why we must be strong and learn to let go
Move on with our lives and go with God's flow
Because He always has a plan for us
And if we look forward and not back and learn to trust
We will enjoy more of our days
When we look forward to what God has to display

31. Do I stick to my principles?

Do I stick to my principles? Is the question I must ask
When I look at the man or woman in the glass
Am I being true to myself? Am I the real McCoy?
Or am I ignoring my conscience and letting my soul be destroyed?

God gave us all a conscience that we must listen to
It will direct us regarding which is the right or wrong thing to do
When we trust it good things come to fruition
But when we don't listen with guilt we are ridden
Nobody is perfect and we all make mistakes
And if we are sorry God will give us a break
But if we continue to ignore His voice inside
Heartache we will cause and tears will occupy our eyes

Refrain

God wants us to do the right things
And listen to Him so a joyous song we will sing
Because when we do good we feel good about ourselves
But when we do wrong guilt is what is felt
Life is short and we have a decision to make
we can't serve two masters so one is at stake
Do we serve the higher good or the lesser evil
Do we take the higher road or the one that makes us feeble

Refrain

Sticking to our principles is not an easy thing to do
Especially when the roar of the crowd is upon you
But if we listen to our conscience and the right choices we make
In the end we will feel good inside and not empty because ourselves we forsake
So when we are confronted with a choice to make
We must remember all the answers lie within and the high road is the one to take

32. Kiss

Keep is simple sweet heart life doesn't need to be complicated
Just follow the leader because His words will never be outdated
Do your best to live in love and you will be ok
And you only have to do it just for today

Life can be confusing at times
It can get complicated when we over think in our minds
But if we sit back and relax
And meditate on how Jesus taught us to act
We will get our answers in regards of the right thing to do
And if we don't know we can pray to Him too
And He will show us how to be
Even though the task at hand might not be so easy

Refrain

When life gets scary and times get hard
We want to look for an easier way but we never get that far
We can't think our way around a resolution
The only way is to go through with the solution
And never is it easy doing the right thing
But in the long run joy it brings
And if we keep it simple we will discover
Things turn out for the best than if we let our minds get cluttered

Refrain

Life can be as simple or as complicated as we want
But do we want to live in peace our let our thoughts haunt
Because living in the mind might at first seem fine
But after a while we feel caught in a bind
So the best thing we can do is not aggravate ourselves
And make mountains out of molehills when pressure is felt
All we have to do is keep it simple sweat heart by following His lead
And whatever the problem we will get what we need

33. Christian leaders

A Christian leader is one who influences others to act
Is willing to be put down and laughed at
Is the one willing to do the will of the Lord
So He can be a fisher of men who fell overboard

It is not easy to proclaim the word
It is even harder to live it so it can be heard
There is a time to preach and a time to teach
And a time to reach out and wash another's feet
And to do our best must be the aim
To help others that are in pain
And claim the hearts of the tortured souls
That they too can be brought in from the cold

Refrain

Our job as Christian leaders
Is to be examples of God's love so when people read us
They know that we are for real
Because they see the light when we speak of our past ordeals
And how God gave us a brand new life
Forgave us for our sins and restored our sight
And showed us the way the truth and the life
That brought us from the darkness and into the light

Refrain

Jesus is who we look to for inspiration
As we go through the stations of the cross there is no hesitation
To think if He could endure His passion I can endure mine
With the help of others who are loving, caring and kind
And though the road less traveled is hard God will give us the courage and the strength
To carry our cross because He never gives us more than we can take
and as we enjoy the life we are called to live
we show our gratitude by being Christian leaders and having hearts that give

34. God wants us to listen

God wants us to listen when He speaks
His words come from way down deep
In our soul where the truth is told
So we must pay attention so we know in which direction to go

G.o.d. is also known as Good. Orderly. Direction.
He loves us so much and deep is His affection
So He talks to us and listens to our pleas
And will help us out with anything we need
But when we ask Him to help us carry our cross
We must remember it's a two-way street and if we don't want to get lost
We need to follow His directions
Because He knows which way to go when we are stuck at an intersection

Refrain

God can speak to us in many ways
He talks through others or put signs on display
He will do whatever it takes to get our attention
And to get us out of our detention
And back in school so we are nobody's fool
And if we listen to the teacher that doesn't misrule
But shows us the right way
We will be on the road to better and brighter days

Refrain

So we must listen when He speaks
Because if we don't we will become obsolete
Our lives will be a living Hell
And in pain and suffering we will dwell
But if we listen to Him we will feel good inside
Our faith will grow and fear will subside
Dreams and goals will be realized
If we open up our ears to His love and ignore all the devils lies
And despise all the evil within
So we can have victory over deceiving sin

35. Bloom where you're planted

Bloom where you're planted take in the sunlight glow
Absorb all the water and watch yourself grow
Into the person you meant to be
Like a mustard seed into a shrub that matures beautifully

God has us where we are for a reason
And we experience various types of seasons
Sometimes it's warm and sometimes it's cold
But in the end both will shape and mold
Us into the person that God wants us to be
So we can be of service to all those in need
And be instruments of His peace
To those pain and suffering will begin to cease

Refrain

It takes time to grow
And the process can be very slow
But if we our patient with ourselves and with God
We will become strong because our roots were strong under the sod
But if we try to rush and want instant gratification overnight
We become frustrated and lose our sight
Of why we are going through this in the first place
Which is to become servants whose purpose is to learn God's way and pace

Refrain

God has a plan and a design
So He can cultivate us and we can become refined
It might take time or it might happen fast
But whatever our schedule is He wants our roots to grasp
And hold onto Him so we rise and shine
And become a vine of the Divine
So we must let the Gardner have His way
And prune us in to what He wants to display
And if we stay in Him and learn to let go
Of the branches that we don't need fruit will grow
And if do we will bloom where we are planted
And sow seeds because we made others enchanted

36. Life in God's friendship

Life in God's friendship is about giving and receiving love
It is honest communication with the Lord above
Who cares for us and provides for our needs
All we have to do is communicate and He will answer our pleas

God is Our Father and also our Friend
He loves us dearly and like the sheppard He will tend to His flock with no end
And if one gets lost and goes astray
He will do everything in His power to have it returned safely
And upon return He will only rejoice
Because His sheep responded to His voice
And made the choice to repent from sin
Making all in Heaven happy for even just one victorious win

Refrain

God is love and He cares for us
His love is unconditional and He adores us
And when we let God be God and us be us
We attain a relationship that is harmonious
There is peace in our hearts when we abide
And live in love and defy the other side
Our souls will feel light and free
When we surrender and develop a relationship that is based on honesty

Refrain

God is our best friend and has a great sense of humor
And wants us to be gentle on ourselves especially when we have our bloopers
Because God knows we aren't perfect and we are born to make mistakes
They serve a purpose making us humble and cause us to depend on Him when our hearts begin to ache
And we might get angry and voice our frustrations inside
But He always forgives and understand it's a tough ride
So matter how much we slip and slide
He is there to pick us up and guide us until we get to the other side

37. Prayer changes people and people change things

Prayer changes people and people change things
And when God enters the heart of a human being what joy it brings
Because when our hearts change so do our minds
And we begin to think like Christ and become loving, caring and kind

Prayer is the most powerful spiritual tool in the universe
When we use it correctly things go to better from worse
Prayer has the ability to change a life
To make one walking in the dark step into the light
Miracles happen each and every day
And they are started when we begin to pray
So if we have something to say to our loving Lord
It should be to help someone get back in accord

Refrain

With God all things are possible
There is nothing too big everything is feasible
He can change a person drastically
And have that person go to from A to Z
It might take time and progress might be slow
Or it might be fast like the wind that blows
But if our direction is aimed at Him
We are sure to be destined to win

Refrain

When God comes into a person's heart
And Grace gives them a brand new start
Gratitude overflows in the mind
And that person that was lost is now easy to find
And as they follow the signs and the Lord's lead
Peace enters their life and old wounds start to heal that used to bleed
Seeds planted long ago begin to sow
And happiness they begin to know
And as they are transformed we see and believe
That prayer changes people and it leads to people changing things

38. To be a Christian

To be a Christian is to be loving, caring and kind
And though we get angry we must forgive all the time
It is to take the road less traveled where we must turn the other cheek
And to be of service to all those that seek

Christ is our example of how we should live
How He loved others and always had it in His heart to forgive
He would give all that He had even His life
To provide salvation and guide those who were lost in the dark back into the light
He suffered and died and had His falls
But was victorious in His resurrection and answering Our Father's call
He accepted His will with Grace
And paid the price for the sins of the human race

Refrain

God loved us so much He gave up His one and only son
And gave Him work to be done
And we could apply this in our own lives
Determining which battles does God want us to fight
God has given us each unique talents to use
To serve Him and each other and spread the Good News
So we must choose to take up our cross
And be like Christ and accept the will of the Boss

Refrain

To be a Christian is simple but hard to do
And we are going to have to depend on Our Father to follow through
And if we are humble enough to ask for the courage and the strength
We will be able to go the extra mile and finish the race
And at the end will be the beginning of Heaven
Where loved family and friends never have to say goodbye again
And we will experience love that will never cease
If we only let go and follow the Prince of Peace

39. An isolated Christian is paralyzed

We are not meant to be alone we are born to be together
And when we work, pray and play all things are better
And an isolated Christian is paralyzed all by themselves
That is why we need each other to nurture and to help

We are part of a community that shares the same belief
That Christ was the savior of our body who provided relief
He took away our sins and freed us from guilt
But He did not do this alone but with people His church He built
There were numerous people that helped Him along the way
Like Simon who helped Him carry His cross to Calvary
And if Christ needed help who are we to think we can do it alone
Pride being the greatest sin is the one we need to stone
And humble ourselves and be part of the ministry
And play our parts like it was a symphony
Because everyone is an instrument in this beautiful song we sing
And when we work together it is better when we are in sync

Refrain

Being alone leads to desperation and fear
And the only thing that can make it disappear
Is coming out of isolation and asking God for help
And being with your brothers and sisters who have felt
The same way at different parts of their lives
Only coming to realize they are only the devils lies
And that we are never alone and we are loved beyond measure
We are God's treasure who from He derives much pleasure
Especially when we are working and playing together

Refrain

God's dream is that all may be one
He wants us together living in peace under the sun
And if we listen to Him and let Him guide
Miracles can happen if we are willing to abide
So we must do our best to be part of the team
Make our contribution and help those in need
And if we do the light will shine on through
And we will no longer be paralyzed but able to walk on and pursue
God's will for us until the end of time
And if we do it together we will get to the top of the mountain we climb

40. Be true (Live like God)

We must be true and live like God
And be loving and caring to those hearts that throb
Because when we are an instrument of His peace
And focus on others we will find a joyous release

Jesus set the example of how we should live
How to carry our cross and how to give
Also how to forgive and love our enemies
Not just seven times but seventy times seven until there is a remedy
And to be true to ourselves is to be true to Christ
Because when we surrender to His will and do not fight
The true self emerges and we become the best that we can be
And in the end the result is that our actions made us happy

Refrain

When we are true to ourselves peace is felt
But sometimes we get confused and lose ourselves
But we have to lose ourselves first in order to find
And when we do we come back stronger in time
God has a plan and knows what we need
He has a time table so there's no need to rush and plead
He knows what is best and what we need to grow
And in His time the person He created us to be will begin to show

Refrain

When we are true and live like God
There are spiritual rewards that leave us awed
When we experience His Grace and it will put a smile on our face
and we learn to appreciate life and enjoy it at a steady pace
Taking everything in stride and learning how to have fun
Relishing every moment until victory is won
And we make it to the Kingdom and have everlasting life
We will thank God for teaching us to be true and giving us the ability to live like

Closing,

This Little Light Of Mine,

This Little Light Of Mine,
I'm going to let it shine
Oh, this little light of mine
I'm going to let it shine

This little light of mine
I'm going to let it shine
Let it shine, all the time, let it shine

All around the neighborhood
I'm going to let it shine
All around the neighborhood
I'm going to let it shine
All around the neighborhood

I'm going to let it shine
Let it shine, all the time, let it shine.
Hide it under a bushel? No!
I'm going to let it shine

Hide it under a bushel? No!
I'm going to let it shine
Hide it under a bushel? No!
I'm going to let it shine
Let it shine, all the time, let it shine.

Don't let Satan [blow] it out!
I'm going to let it shine
Don't let Satan [blow] it out!
I'm going to let it shine
Don't let Satan [blow] it out!
I'm going to let it shine
Let it shine, all the time, let it shine

When The Saints Go Marching In,

Oh, when the saints go marching in
Oh, when the saints go marching in
Oh Lord I want to be in that number
When the saints go marching in.

Oh, when the drums begin to bang
Oh, when the drums begin to bang
Oh Lord I want to be in that number
When the saints go marching in.

Oh, when the stars fall from the sky
Oh, when the stars fall from the sky
Oh Lord I want to be in that number
When the saints go marching in.

Oh, when the moon turns red with blood
Oh, when the moon turns red with blood
Oh Lord I want to be in that number
When the saints go marching in.

Oh, when the trumpet sounds its call
Oh, when the trumpet sounds its call
Oh Lord I want to be in that number
When the saints go marching in.

Oh, when the horsemen begin to ride
Oh, when the horsemen begin to ride
Oh Lord I want to be in that number
When the saints go marching in.

Oh, brother Charles you are my friend
Oh, brother Charles you are my friend
Yea, you gonna be in that number
When the saints go marching in.

Oh, when the saints go marching in
Oh, when the saints go marching in
Oh Lord I want to be in that number
When the saints go marching in.

DeColores!,

"DeColores!" is Spanish for "In Colors!" or "To be in God's Grace". The phrase is used to greet fellow cursillistas. The tradition started in the movement's formative days when a group of men from Majorca, Spain were returning from their Cursillo and their bus broke down. They began to sing "DeColores!" which was a traditional folk song and it spread throughout the Spanish speaking world and beyond.

The multi-color rooster that is the symbol for the Cursillo movement was believed to be derived from this song.

De colores, de colores

Se visten los campos en la primavera.

De colores, de colores

Son los pajaritos que vienen de afuera.

De colores, de colores

Es el arco iris que vemos lucir.

Y por eso los grandes amores

De muchos colores me gustan a mi.

Y por eso los grandes amores

De muchos colores me gustan a mi.

De colores, de colores

Brillantes y finos se viste la aurora.

De colores, de colores

Son los mil reflejos que el sol atesora.

De colores, de colores

Se viste el diamante que vemos lucir.

Y por eso los grandes amores

De muchos colores me gustan a mi.

Y por eso los grandes amores

De muchos colores me gustan a mi.

Canta el gallo, canta el gallo

Con el quiri, quiri, quiri, quiri, quiri.

La gallina, la gallina

Con el cara, cara, cara, cara, cara.

Los pollitos/polluelos, los pollitos/polluelos

Con el pio, pio, pio, pio, pi.

Y por eso los grandes amores

De muchos colores me gustan a mi.

Y por eso los grandes amores

De muchos colores me gustan a mi.

Jubilosos, jubilosos

Vivamos en gracia puesto que se puede.

Saciaremos, saciaremos

La sed ardorosa del Rey que no muere.

Jubilosos, jubilosos

Llevemos a Cristo un alma y mil más.

Difundiendo la luz que ilumina

La gracia divina del gran ideal.

Difundiendo la luz que ilumina

La gracia divina del gran ideal.

De colores, de colores

Ultreya! How's your 4th day?

How's your 4th day and the rest of your life?
Have you thanked Jesus for restoring your sight?
Giving you the eyes and ability to see
All the goodness in yourself and all of humanity
And delivering you from the darkness and into the light
To the road less traveled the only one that's right?
It might be a hard fight but it's the way to go
And even though progress at times maybe painfully slow
If you keep on moving forward soon you will be
The person that God created you to be
So hang in there when times get tough
And ask for the courage and the strength when you feel you have had enough
And God will provide everything you need
All you have to do is take a knee and ask humbly
And if you make it your aim to serve and please
And help all of those that are in need
When your work is done He will gently call you home
Where peace is eternal and the Saints and the Angels rome.

About the Author

Ryan made his Cursillo in January of 2006 with group 196. After struggling with his Faith for a number of years "The Cursillo" was instrumental in bringing Ryan back to the Faith of his youth. Out of gratitude Ryan wanted to give back to the movement that changed the course of his life so he took 40 of the topics discussed on the weekend and converted them into Hip Hop Poetry songs in the hope that he would inspire and uplift others like others had done for him.

Thecursillohowsyour4thday.com

"In everything give thanks: for this is the will of God in Christ Jesus concerning you."
1 Thessalonians 5:18

Thy
will
be
done!

Printed in the United States
by Baker & Taylor Publisher Services